be kept

WINTER WORDS

IN VARIOUS MOODS AND METRES

THE MACMILLAN COMPANY
NEW YORK · BOSTON · CHICAGO · DALLAS
ATLANTA · SAN FRANCISCO

MACMILLAN & CO., Limited
LONDON · BOMBAY · CALCUTTA
MELBOURNE

THE MACMILLAN CO. OF CANADA, Ltd.
TORONTO

WINTER WORDS

IN VARIOUS MOODS AND METRES

BY

THOMAS HARDY

THE MACMILLAN COMPANY

NEW YORK   MCMXXIX

COPYRIGHT, 1928,

'BY FLORENCE E. HARDY AND SYDNEY E. COCKERELL

———

Set up and electrotyped. Published November, 1928. Reprinted
November, 1928; January, 1929.

Norwood Press
J. S. Cushing Co. — Berwick & Smith Co.
Norwood, Mass., U.S.A.

[This volume, though prepared for the press, would have undergone further revision, had the author lived to issue it on the birthday of which he left the number uninserted below.]

INTRODUCTORY NOTE

So far as I am aware, I happen to be the only English poet who has brought out a new volume of his verse on his . . . birthday, whatever may have been the case with the ancient Greeks, for it must be remembered that poets did not die young in those days.

This, however, is not the point of the present few preliminary words. My last volume of poems was pronounced wholly gloomy and pessimistic by reviewers — even by some of the more able class. My sense of the oddity of this verdict may be imagined when, in selecting them, I had been, as I thought, rather too liberal in admitting flippant, not to say farcical, pieces into the collection. However, I did not suppose that the licensed tasters had wilfully misrepresented the book, and said nothing, knowing well that they could not have read it.

INTRODUCTORY NOTE

As labels stick, I foresee readily enough that the same perennial inscription will be set on the following pages, and therefore take no trouble to argue on the proceeding, notwithstanding the surprises to which I could treat my critics by uncovering a place here and there to them in the volume.

This being probably my last appearance on the literary stage, I would say, more seriously, that though, alas, it would be idle to pretend that the publication of these poems can have much interest for me, the track having been adventured so many times before to-day, the pieces themselves have been prepared with reasonable care, if not quite with the zest of a young man new to print.

I also repeat what I have often stated on such occasions, that no harmonious philosophy is attempted in these pages — or in any bygone pages of mine, for that matter.

T. H.

CONTENTS

CONTENTS

CONTENTS

CONTENTS

CONTENTS

xi

THE NEW DAWN'S BUSINESS

WHAT are you doing outside my walls,
    O Dawn of another day?
I have not called you over the edge
    Of the heathy ledge,
    So why do you come this way,
With your furtive footstep without sound
    here,
    And your face so deedily gray?

"I show a light for killing the man
    Who lives not far from you,
And for bringing to birth the lady's child,
    Nigh domiciled,
    And for earthing a corpse or two,
And for several other such odd jobs round
    here
    That Time to-day must do.

"But you he leaves alone (although,
    As you have often said,
You are always ready to pay the debt
    You don't forget
    You owe for board and bed :)
The truth is, when men willing are found here
    He takes those loth instead."

I

PROUD SONGSTERS

THE thrushes sing as the sun is going,
　　And the finches whistle in ones and
　　　　pairs,
And as it gets dark loud nightingales
　　　　In bushes
Pipe, as they can when April wears,
　　As if all Time were theirs.

These are brand new birds of twelve-months'
　　　　growing,
Which a year ago, or less than twain,
No finches were, nor nightingales,
　　　　Nor thrushes,
But only particles of grain,
　　And earth, and air, and rain.

THOUGHTS AT MIDNIGHT

MANKIND, you dismay me
   When shadows waylay me! —
Not by your splendours
Do you affray me,
Not as pretenders
To demonic keenness,
Not by your meanness,
Nor your ill-teachings,
Nor your false preachings,
Nor your banalities
And immoralities,
Nor by your daring
Nor sinister bearing;
But by your madnesses
Capping cool badnesses,
Acting like puppets
Under Time's buffets;
In superstitions
And ambitions
Moved by no wisdom,

3

THOUGHTS AT MIDNIGHT

Far-sight, or system,
Led by sheer senselessness
And presciencelessness
Into unreason
And hideous self-treason. . . .
God, look he on you,
Have mercy upon you!

Part written 25th May 1906.

4

"I AM THE ONE"

I AM the one whom ringdoves see
    Through chinks in boughs
    When they do not rouse
    In sudden dread,
But stay on cooing, as if they said :
    "Oh ; it's only he."

I am the passer when up-eared hares,
    Stirred as they eat
    The new-sprung wheat,
    Their munch resume
As if they thought : "He is one for whom
    Nobody cares."

Wet-eyed mourners glance at me
    As in train they pass
    Along the grass
    To a hollowed spot,
And think : "No matter ; he quizzes not
    Our misery."

"I AM THE ONE"

I hear above: "We stars must lend
    No fierce regard
    To his gaze, so hard
    Bent on us thus, —
Must scathe him not.   He is one with us
    Beginning and end."

THE PROPHETESS

1

"NOW shall I sing
    That pretty thing
'The   Mocking-Bird'?" — And   sing   it
    straight did she.
    I had no cause
    To think it was
A Mocking-bird in truth that sang to me.

2

    Not even the glance
    She threw askance
Foretold to me, nor did the tune or rhyme,
    That the words bore
    A meaning more
Than that they were a ditty of the time.

3

    But after years
    Of hopes and fears,
And all they bring, and all they take away,
    I found I had heard
    The Mocking-bird
In person singing there to me that day.

A WISH FOR UNCONSCIOUSNESS

IF I could but abide
  As a tablet on a wall,
Or a hillock daisy-pied,
Or a picture in a hall,
And as nothing else at all,
I should feel no doleful achings,
I should hear no judgment-call,
Have no evil dreams or wakings,
No uncouth or grisly care;
In a word, no cross to bear.

THE BAD EXAMPLE

FIE, Aphrodite, shamming you are no
    mother,
And your maternal markings trying to
    smother,
As you were maiden, now you love
    another ! . . .
If one like you need such pretence to noose
    him,
Indulgence in too early fires beware you,
All girls yet virgin, and have constant care
    you
Become not staled by use as she has, ere
    you
Meet your most-loved ; lest, tumbled, you
    should lose him.

Partly from Meleager.

TO LOUISA IN THE LANE

MEET me again as at that time
   In the hollow of the lane;
I will not pass as in my prime
   I passed at each day's wane.
     — Ah, I remember!
To do it you will have to see
Anew this sorry scene wherein you have
     ceased to be!

But I will welcome your aspen form
   As you gaze wondering round
And say with spectral frail alarm,
   "Why am I still here found?
     — Ah, I remember!
It is through him with blitheful brow
Who did not love me then, but loves and
     draws me now!"

10

TO LOUISA IN THE LANE

And I shall answer: "Sweet of eyes,
    Carry me with you, Dear,
To where you donned this spirit-guise;
    It's better there than here!"
      — Till I remember
Such is a deed you cannot do:
Wait must I, till with flung-off flesh I follow
      you.

LOVE WATCHES A WINDOW

" HERE   in   the   window   beaming
              across
Is he — the lineaments like him so! —
The saint whose name I do not know,
With the holy robe and the cheek aglow.
Here will I kneel as if worshipping God
When all the time I am worshipping you,
              Whose Love I was —
You that with me will nevermore tread anew
              The paradise-paths we trod!"

She came to that prominent pew each
        day,
And sat there.   Zealously she came
And watched her Love — looking just the
        same
From the rubied eastern tracery-frame —
The man who had quite forsaken her
And followed another, it was thought. —
              Be't as it may,
Thinner, more thin, was the lady's figure
        wrought
              By some ache, year on year.

12

LOVE WATCHES A WINDOW

Well, now she's dead, and dead is he
From whom her heart once drew delight,
Whose face glowed daily, lover-bright,
High in the glass before her sight.
And still the face is seen as clear
In the rubied eastern window-gleam
      As formerly ;
But not seen now is a passioned woman's
    dream
      Glowing beside it there.

THE LOVE–LETTERS

(IN MEMORIAM H. R.)

I MET him quite by accident
  In a bye-path that he'd frequent.
And, as he neared, the sunset glow
Warmed up the smile of pleasantry
Upon his too thin face, while he
Held a square packet up to me,
    Of what, I did not know.

"Well," said he then; "they are my old
    letters.
Perhaps she — rather felt them fetters. . . .
You see, I am in a slow decline,
And she's broken off with me.   Quite right
To send them back, and true foresight;
I'd got too fond of her!   To-night
    I burn them — stuff of mine!"

He laughed in the sun — an ache in his
    laughter —
And went.   I heard of his death soon after.

14

AN UNKINDLY MAY

A SHEPHERD stands by a gate in a
white smock-frock:
He holds the gate ajar, intently counting his
flock.

The sour spring wind is blurting boisterous-
wise,
And bears on it dirty clouds across the skies;
Plantation timbers creak like rusty cranes,
And pigeons and rooks, dishevelled by late
rains,
Are like gaunt vultures, sodden and unkempt,
And song-birds do not end what they
attempt:
The buds have tried to open, but quite
failing
Have pinched themselves together in their
quailing.
The sun frowns whitely in eye-trying flaps
Through passing cloud-holes, mimicking
audible taps.
"Nature, you're not commendable to-day!"
I think. "Better to-morrow!" she seems
to say.

AN UNKINDLY MAY

That shepherd still stands in that white
  smock-frock,
Unnoting all things save the counting his
  flock.

UNKEPT GOOD FRIDAYS

THERE are many more Good Fridays
   Than this, if we but knew
The names, and could relate them,
   Of men whom rulers slew
For their goodwill, and date them
   As runs the twelvemonth through.

These nameless Christs' Good Fridays,
   Whose virtues wrought their end,
Bore days of bonds and burning,
   With no man to their friend,
Of mockeries, and spurning ;
   Yet they are all unpenned.

When they had their Good Fridays
   Of bloody sweat and strain
Oblivion hides.   We quote not
   Their dying words of pain,
Their sepulchres we note not,
   Unwitting where they have lain.

No annual Good Fridays
   Gained they from cross and cord,

UNKEPT GOOD FRIDAYS

From being sawn asunder,
   Disfigured and abhorred,
Smitten and trampled under:
   Such dates no hands have scored.

Let be.   Let lack Good Fridays
   These Christs of unwrit names;
The world was not even worthy
   To taunt their hopes and aims,
As little of earth, earthy,
   As his mankind proclaims.

Good Friday, 1927.

THE MOUND

FOR a moment pause : —
　　Just here it was ;
And through the thin thorn hedge, by the
　　rays of the moon,
I can see the tree in the field, and beside it the
　　mound —
Now sheeted with snow — whereon we sat
　　that June
　　When it was green and round,
And she crazed my mind by what she coolly
　　told —
　　The history of her undoing,
(As I saw it), but she called "comradeship,"
　　That bred in her no rueing :
　　And saying she'd not be bound
For life to one man, young, ripe-yeared, or
　　old,
Left me — an innocent simpleton to her
　　viewing ;
For, though my accompt of years outscored
　　her own,
　　Hers had more hotly flown. . . .
We never met again by this green mound,
To press as once so often lip on lip,
　　　And palter, and pause : —
　　　Yes ; here it was !

LIDDELL AND SCOTT

ON THE COMPLETION OF THEIR LEXICON

(Written after the death of Liddell in 1898.
Scott had died some ten years earlier.)

" WELL, though it seems
      Beyond our dreams,"
Said Liddell to Scott,
"We've really got
To the very end,
All inked and penned
Blotless and fair
Without turning a hair,
This sultry summer day, A.D.
Eighteen hundred and forty-three.

"I've often, I own,
Belched many a moan
At undertaking it,
And dreamt forsaking it.
— Yes, on to Pi,
When the end loomed nigh,
And friends said : 'You've as good as done,'
I almost wished we'd not begun.

LIDDELL AND SCOTT

Even now, if people only knew
My sinkings, as we slowly drew
Along through Kappa, Lambda, Mu,
They'd be concerned at my misgiving,
And how I mused on a College living
      Right down to Sigma,
      But feared a stigma
If I succumbed, and left old Donnegan
For weary freshmen's eyes to con again :
And how I often, often wondered
What could have led me to have blundered
So far away from sound theology
To dialects and etymology ;
Words, accents not to be breathed by men
Of any country ever again !"

      "My heart most failed,
      Indeed, quite quailed,"
    Said Scott to Liddell,
    "Long ere the middle ! . . .
     Twas one wet dawn
    When, slippers on,
    And a cold in the head anew,
    Gazing at Delta
    I turned and felt a
    Wish for bed anew,
    And to let supersedings
    Of Passow's readings

In dialects go.
'That German has read
More than we!' I said;
Yea, several times did I feel so! . . .

"O that first morning, smiling bland,
With sheets of foolscap, quills in hand,
To write ἀάατος and ἀαγής,
Followed by fifteen hundred pages,
What nerve was ours
So to back our powers,
Assured that we should reach ὠώδης
While there was breath left in our bodies!"

Liddell replied: "Well, that's past now;
The job's done, thank God, anyhow."

"And yet it's not,"
Considered Scott,
"For we've to get
Subscribers yet
We must remember;
Yes; by September."

"O Lord; dismiss that. We'll succeed.
Dinner is my immediate need.
I feel as hollow as a fiddle,
Working so many hours," said Liddell.

CHRISTMASTIDE

THE rain-shafts splintered on me
  As despondently I strode;
The twilight gloomed upon me
  And bleared the blank high-road.
Each bush gave forth, when blown on
  By gusts in shower and shower,
A sigh, as it were sown on
  In handfuls by a sower.

A cheerful voice called, nigh me,
  "A merry Christmas, friend!" —
There rose a figure by me,
  Walking with townward trend,
A sodden tramp's, who, breaking
  Into thin song, bore straight
Ahead, direction taking
  Toward the Casuals' gate.

RELUCTANT CONFESSION

"WHAT did you do? Cannot you let me
    know?"
"Don't ask! . . . 'Twas midnight, and I'd
    lost at cards."
"Ah. Was it crime — or seemed it to be
    so?"
    "No — not till afterwards."
    "But *what*, then, did you do?"
"Well — that was the beginning — months
    ago;
You see, I had lost, and could not pay
    but — so.
And there flashed from him strange and
    strong regards
That you only see when scruples smash to
    shards;
And thus it happened — O it rained and
    blew! —
But I can't tell. 'Twas all so lurid in hue!
And what was worst came after, when I knew
    What first crossed not my mind,
    And he has never divined!" . . .
"But he must have, if he proposed it you?"

RELUCTANT CONFESSION

"I mean, that — I got rid of what resulted
In a way a woman told me I consulted :
    'Tis that he does not know ;
    Great God, it harrows me so !
    I did not mean to.   Every night —
        In hell-dark dreams
    I see an appealing figure in white —
        That somehow seems
A newborn child in the clothes I set to make,
But left off, for my own depraved name's
      sake !"

EXPECTATION AND EXPERIENCE

"I HAD a holiday once," said the woman —
    Her name I did not know —
"And I thought that where I'd like to go,
Of all the places for being jolly,
And getting rid of melancholy,
    Would be to a good big fair:
And I went. And it rained in torrents,
        drenching
Every horse, and sheep, and yeoman,
    And my shoulders, face and hair;
And I found that I was the single woman
    In the field — and looked quite odd there!
Everything was spirit-quenching:
I crept and stood in the lew of a wall
To think, and could not tell at all
    What on earth made me plod there!"

ARISTODEMUS THE MESSENIAN

(DRAMATIC HENDECASYLLABICS)

SCENE: BEFORE THE STRONGHOLD OF ITHOME, MESSENIA, 735 B.C.

His daughter's lover discovered, in the disguise of a soothsayer; to whom enters ARISTODEMUS.

ARISTODEMUS (*apostrophically*)

Straightway let it be done!

LOVER

      Let what be done, chief?

ARISTODEMUS

Who art thou that art speaking? Some sage
   prophet? —
She, my daughter's to perish on the altar!

LOVER

Thou called hero! — a myth thy vaunted
   power,
If it fail to redeem thy best beloved.

27

ARISTODEMUS THE MESSENIAN

ARISTODEMUS

Power is naught to the matter. What the
Sibyl
Bids, must be!

LOVER

But I doubt such bidding thereto.

ARISTODEMUS

Nay. White lippings above the Delphic
tripod
Mangle never their message! And they lip
such.
Thriving, conquering shall Messene be forth-
with —
Future worthy my gift of this intact one.
Yea, and who of the Aépўtids renowned
house
Weigh can greater with Zeus than she my
offspring?
Shall these Spartiats sway to save me reave-
ment?
What is fatherhood when they march in
hearing?
Hark! E'en now they are here!

(*Marching soldiers heard afar.*)

LOVER (*after a silence*)

And mean you to warn her?

28

ARISTODEMUS THE MESSENIAN

ARISTODEMUS

Not till evening shades can cover pallor.

[Exit.

*Lover stands motionless. Enter the daughter
of* ARISTODEMUS.

DAUGHTER

Ah! Thou comest to me, Love, not as earlier!

*Lover, as it were waking, approaches, un-
hoods his face, and embraces her.*

Why not speak to me?

LOVER

Sweetest, thou'rt a doomed one!

DAUGHTER

How?

LOVER

Thy sacrifice by thy father waits thee —
Thee, as offering for the State's salvation.

DAUGHTER

Not the slaying of me?

LOVER

Fail I to stay him —
(*She droops in his arms*)
Whereto bursts in a flame a means upon me!

29

DAUGHTER

How? My father is mighty. Thou'rt so
    powerless.

LOVER

Thus and now it adumbrates. Haste I to
    him,
Vowing love for thee!

DAUGHTER

        Which he'll value wryly —
Less than naught, as I know.

LOVER

          Till comes my sequel;
This, to wit. Thou art got with child by
    me. Ay,
List: the Sibylline utterance asks a virgin;
So th'rt saved!

DAUGHTER

      But a maid's the thing I am, Love!
Gods! With child I am not, but veriest
    virgin —
Who knows surer than thou?

LOVER

         I'll make him think so,
Though no man upon earth more knows its
    falseness,
Such will I.

DAUGHTER

But alas, thou canst not make him:
Me he knows to the core.   He'll not believe
    thee.

LOVER

Then thou canst.   He'll accept thy vouching,
    sure, Sweet,
And another intact one, equal serving,
Straightway find for the knife.

DAUGHTER

      My Love, I must not!

LOVER

Not?   And yet there is pending for thee,
    elsewise,
Dark destruction, and all thy burning being
Dungeoned in an eternal nescientness!

*She shudders, but weepingly shows unwilling-
    ness.*

Stay.   I'll make the asseverance first.
    Thou'lt clinch it?

DAUGHTER

    (with white cheeks, after a pause)

Be it so! . . .

ARISTODEMUS THE MESSENIAN

The Messenian army is heard going out to meet the Spartans. Lover hoods himself as ARISTODEMUS *enters from the stronghold.*

ARISTODEMUS

(looking strangely at his daughter)

Stay you yet at the gate? The old man also?
Hath indeed he disclosed the sore pronouncement?

DAUGHTER *(falteringly)*

Sore pronouncement? And what is, sire, its substance?

Messenger enters.

MESSENGER

King Euphaes is just found slain in combat:
Thereby King is the Chief, Aristodemus,
E'en ere falters the strife — still hard against us!

ARISTODEMUS

Ha! And is it in balance yet! — The deed, then!

Daughter looks at her lover, who throws off his disguise; and they go up to ARISTODEMUS *together.*

Who's this man? And to what tends all this feigning?

ARISTODEMUS THE MESSENIAN

DAUGHTER

He — my lover — who thinks to be my
    husband —
O my father, thy pardon! Know a secret!

ARISTODEMUS

Lover? Secret? And what? But such is
    naught now:
Husband he nor another can be to thee,
Let him think as he may! And though I
    meant not
Death to broach till the eve, let doom be
    dealt now.
Hark, the Spartan assays! It straight be-
    hoves me,
Cost it what to my soul, to give deliverance
To my country the instant. Thou, my
    daughter,
Foremost maiden of all the maidens round
    us —

DAUGHTER

O but save me, I pray, sire! And to that end
There has now to be spoke a thing immediate,
And I fain would be speaker. But I cannot!
What he now will reveal, receive as vouched
    for!

               (*She rushes into the castle.*)

ARISTODEMUS THE MESSENIAN

ARISTODEMUS (*to lover*)

What means this in her? Reads she what's
    impending?

LOVER

King, its meaning is much! That she's with
    child. Yea,
By me! Hence there is called for immolation
One who's what she is not — a sure-sealed
    virgin —
If you'd haste to deliver stressed Ithome,
Bulking yet overhead as though unweakened!

    ARISTODEMUS *sinks on to a projection of the
    rock, and covers his eyes.*

ARISTODEMUS (*brokenly*)

Better had she been made the purposed
    victim
Than that this should have so befallen to
    save her!
Foul disaster of fatherhood and home-
    pride! . . .
Let this citadel fall; the Spartan army
Trample over its dust, and enter in here!
She is worse than a martyr for the State-weal,
I than one of the slain. And king tomorrow!
                (*He pauses.*)

'Tis not true!

He makes as if to fall upon her lover with his sword. Lover defends himself with his dagger. ARISTODEMUS *turns to rush into the castle after his daughter.*

> I misdoubt it! They speak falsely!
> [*Exit* ARISTODEMUS.

Lover walks up and down in strained suspense. Interval. A groan is heard. Lover is about to rush out, but re-enter ARISTODEMUS *sword in hand, now bloody.*

ARISTODEMUS

I have proved me her honour, shown the
    falsehood
Ye twain both have declared me!

LOVER

That canst not do!

ARISTODEMUS

I say I have outshown it; proved her even
Until death very virgin pure and spotless!
Enter Attendants.

ATTENDANTS (*severally*)

Horror, horror indeed! He's ripped her
    up — yea,

35

With his sword! He hath split her beauteous body
To prove her maid!

ARISTODEMUS (*to lover*)

Now diest thou for thy lying, like as she died!

*He turns his sword on lover, but falls from
exhaustion. Lover seizes* ARISTODEMUS'
*sword, and is about to run him through
with it; but he checks his hand, and turns
the sword upon himself.*

(*Lover dies.*)

EVENING SHADOWS

THE shadows of my chimneys stretch
    afar
Across the plot, and on to the privet bower,
And even the shadows of their smokings
    show,
And nothing says just now that where they
    are
They will in future stretch at this same hour,
Though in my earthen cyst I shall not know.

And at this time the neighbouring Pagan
    mound,
Whose myths the Gospel news now super-
    sede,
Upon the greensward also throws its shade,
And nothing says such shade will spread
    around
Even as to-day when men will no more heed
The Gospel news than when the mound was
    made.

THE THREE TALL MEN

The First Tapping

"WHAT'S that tapping at night: tack, tack,
In some house in the street at the back?"

"O, 'tis a man who, when he has leisure,
Is making himself a coffin to measure.
He's so very tall that no carpenter
Will make it long enough, he's in fear.
His father's was shockingly short for his
  limb —
And it made a deep impression on him."

The Second Tapping

"That tapping has begun again,
Which ceased a year back, or near then?"

"Yes, 'tis the man you heard before
Making his coffin.   The first scarce done
His brother died — his only one —
And, being of his own height, or more,
He used it for him; for he was afraid
He'd not get a long enough one quick made.

THE THREE TALL MEN

He's making a second now, to fit
Himself when there shall be need for it.
Carpenters work so by rule of thumb
That they make mistakes when orders come."

THE THIRD TAPPING

"It's strange, but years back, when I was
    here,
I used to notice a tapping near;
A man was making his coffin at night,
And he made a second, if I am right?
I have heard again the self-same tapping —
Yes, late last night — or was I napping?"

"O no. It's the same man. He made one
Which his brother had; and a second was
    done —
For himself, as he thought. But lately his
    son,
As tall as he, died; aye, and as trim,
And his sorrowful father bestowed it on him.
And now the man is making a third,
To be used for himself when he is interred."

"Many years later was brought to me
News that the man had died at sea."

THE LODGING–HOUSE FUCHSIAS

MRS. MASTERS'S fuchsias hung
    Higher   and   broader,   and   brightly
      swung,
    Bell-like, more and more
Over the narrow garden-path,
Giving the passer a sprinkle-bath
      In the morning.

She put up with their pushful ways,
And made us tenderly lift their sprays,
      Going to her door:
But when her funeral had to pass
They cut back all the flowery mass
      In the morning.

THE WHALER'S WIFE

I NEVER pass that inn "The Ring of
Bells"
Without recalling what its signpost tells
        To recollection:
A tale such as all houses yield, maybe,
That ever have known of fealties, phantasy,
        Hate, or affection.

He has come from a whaling cruise to settle
    down
As publican in his small native town,
        Where his wife dwells.
It is a Sunday morning; she has gone
To church with others. Service still being
    on,
        He seeks "The Bells."

"Yes: she's quite thriving; very much so,
        they say.
I don't believe in tales; 'tis not my way!
        I hold them stuff.
But — as you press me — certainly we know
He visits her once at least each week or so,
        Fair weather or rough.

41

"And, after all, he's quite a gentleman,
And lonely wives must friend them where
    they can.
        She'll tell you all,
No doubt, when prayers are done and she
    comes home.
I'm glad to hear your early taste to roam
        Begins to pall."

"I'll stroll out and await her," then said he.
Anon the congregation passed, and she
        Passed with the rest,
Unconscious of the great surprise at hand
And bounding on, and smiling — fair and
    bland —
        In her Sunday best.

Straight she was told. She fainted at the
    news,
But rallied, and was able to refuse
        Help to her home.
There she sat waiting all day — with a
    look —
A look of joy, it seemed, if none mistook . . .
        But he did not come.

Time flew : her husband kept him absent
    still,

THE WHALER'S WIFE

And by slow slips the woman pined, until,
    Grown thin, she died —
Of grief at loss of him, some would aver,
But how could that be? They anyway
    buried her
        By her mother's side.

And by the grave stood, at the funeral,
A tall man, elderly and grave withal;
        Gossip grew grim:
He was the same one who had been seen
    before;
He paid, in cash, all owing; and no more
        Was heard of him.

At the pulling down of her house, decayed
    and old,
Many years after, was the true tale told
        By an ancient swain.
The tall man was the father of the
    wife.
He had beguiled her mother in maiden
    life,
        And to cover her stain,

Induced to wive her one in his service bred,
Who brought her daughter up as his till
    wed.

THE WHALER'S WIFE

— This the girl knew,
But hid it close, to save her mother's name,
Even from her seaman spouse, and ruined
    her fame
      With him, though true.

THROWING A TREE

NEW FOREST

THE two executioners stalk along
    over the knolls,
Bearing two axes with heavy heads
    shining and wide,
And a long limp two-handled saw
    toothed for cutting great boles,
And so they approach the proud tree that
    bears the death-mark on its side.

Jackets doffed they swing axes and chop
    away just above ground,
And the chips fly about and lie white on
    the moss and fallen leaves ;
Till a broad deep gash in the bark is
    hewn all the way round,
And one of them tries to hook upward a rope,
    which at last he achieves.

The saw then begins, till the top of the
    tall giant shivers :
The shivers are seen to grow greater each
    cut than before :

45

THROWING A TREE

They edge out the saw, tug the rope;
      but the tree only quivers,
And kneeling and sawing again, they step
      back to try pulling once more.

Then, lastly, the living mast sways,
      further sways: with a shout
Job and Ike rush aside. Reached the
      end of its long staying powers
The tree crashes downward: it shakes
      all its neighbours throughout,
And two hundred years' steady growth has
      been ended in less than two hours.

THE WAR–WIFE OF CATKNOLL

"WHAT crowd is this in Catknoll Street,
      Now I am just come home?
What crowd is this in my old street,
      That flings me such a glance?
A   stretcher — and   corpse? A   sobering
      sight
To greet me, when my heart is light
With thoughts of coming cheer to-night
      Now I am back from France."

"O 'tis a woman, soldier-man,
      Who seems to be new come:
O 'tis a woman, soldier-man,
      Found in the river here,
Whither she went and threw her in,
And now they are carrying her within:
She's drowned herself for a sly sin
      Against her husband dear.

" 'A said to me, who knew her well,
      'O why was I so weak!'
'A said to me, who knew her well,
      And have done all her life,

47

With a downcast face she said to me,
'O why did I keep company
Wi' them that practised gallantry,
  When vowed a faithful wife!'

" 'O God, I'm driven mad!' she said,
  'To hear he's coming back;
I'm fairly driven mad!' she said:
  'He's been two years agone,
And now he'll find me in this state,
And not forgive me.   Had but fate
Kept back his coming three months late,
  Nothing of it he'd known!'

"We did not think she meant so much,
  And said; 'He may forgive.'
O never we thought she meant so much
  As to go doing this.
And now she must be crowned! — so fair! —
Who drew men's eyes so everywhere! —
And love-letters beyond compare
  For coaxing to a kiss.

"She kept her true a year or more
  Against the young men all;
Yes, kept her true a year or more,
  And they were most to blame.

There was Will Peach who plays the flute,
And Waywell with the dandy suit,
And Nobb, and Knight. . . . But she's
    been mute
      As to the father's name."

NOTE : verse 5. — " She must be crowned."   Old English
for " there must be a coroner's inquest over her."

CONCERNING HIS OLD HOME

Mood I

I WISH to see it never —
  That dismal place
  With cracks in its floor —
I would forget it ever!

Mood II

To see it once, that sad
  And memoried place —
  Yes, just once more —
I should be faintly glad!

Mood III

To see it often again —
  That friendly place
  With its green low door —
I'm willing anywhen!

Mood IV

I'll haunt it night and day —
  That loveable place,
  With its flowers' rich store
That drives regret away!

50

HER SECOND HUSBAND
HEARS HER STORY

"STILL, Dear, it is incredible to me
        That here, alone,
You should have sewed him up until he died,
And in this very bed.   I do not see
How you could do it, seeing what might
        betide."

"Well, he came home one midnight, liquored
        deep —
        Worse than I'd known —
And lay down heavily, and soundly slept:
Then, desperate driven, I thought of it, to
        keep
Him from me when he woke.   Being an adept

"With needle and thimble, as he snored,
        click-click
        An hour I'd sewn,
Till, had he roused, he couldn't have moved
        from bed,
So tightly laced in sheet and quilt and tick
He lay.   And in the morning he was dead.

51

"Ere people came I drew the stitches out,
    And thus 'twas shown
To be a stroke." — "It's a strange tale!"
    said he.
"And this same bed?" — "Yes, here it
    came about."
"Well, it sounds strange — told here and
    now to me.

"Did you intend his death by your tight
    lacing?"
        "O, that I cannot own.
I could not think of else that would avail
When he should wake up, and attempt em-
    bracing." —
        "Well, it's a cool queer tale!"

YULETIDE IN A YOUNGER WORLD

WE believed in highdays then,
    And could glimpse at night
    On Christmas Eve
Imminent oncomings of radiant revel —
    Doings of delight : —
    Now we have no such sight.

We had eyes for phantoms then,
    And at bridge or stile
    On Christmas Eve
Clear beheld those countless ones who had
        crossed it
    Cross again in file : —
    Such has ceased longwhile !

We liked divination then,
    And, as they homeward wound
    On Christmas Eve,
We could read men's dreams within them
        spinning
    Even as wheels spin round : —
    Now we are blinker-bound.

53

YULETIDE IN A YOUNGER WORLD

We heard still small voices then,
   And, in the dim serene
    Of Christmas Eve,
Caught the fartime tones of fire-filled
    prophets
   Long on earth unseen. . . .
   — Can such ever have been?

AFTER THE DEATH OF
A FRIEND

YOU died, and made but little of it! —
    Why then should I, when called to
        doff it,
Drop, and renounce this worm-holed raiment,
Shrink edgewise off from its gray claimant?
Rather say, when I am Time-outrun,
As you did: Take me, and have done,
Inexorable, insatiate one!

THE SON'S PORTRAIT

I WALKED the streets of a market town,
  And came to a lumber-shop,
Which I had known ere I met the frown
    Of fate and fortune,
  And habit led me to stop.

In burrowing mid this chattel and that,
  High, low, or edgewise thrown,
I lit upon something lying flat —
    A fly-flecked portrait,
  Framed. 'Twas my dead son's own.

"That photo? . . . A lady — I know not
      whence —
  Sold it me, Ma'am, one day,
With more. You can have it for eighteen-
      pence:
    The picture's nothing;
  It's but for the frame you pay."

He had given it her in their heyday shine,
  When she wedded him, long her wooer:

THE SON'S PORTRAIT

And then he was sent to the front-trench-line,
    And fell there fighting ;
  And she took a new bridegroom to her.

I bought the gift she had held so light,
    And *buried it* — as 'twere he. —
Well, well! Such things are trifling, quite,
    But when one's lonely
  How cruel they can be!

LYING AWAKE

YOU, Morningtide Star, now are steady-
        eyed, over the east,
    I know it as if I saw you;
You, Beeches, engrave on the sky your thin
        twigs, even the least;
    Had I paper and pencil I'd draw you.

You, Meadow, are white with your counter-
        pane cover of dew,
    I see it as if I were there;
You, Churchyard, are lightening faint from
        the shade of the yew,
    The names creeping out everywhere.

THE LADY IN THE FURS

"I'M a lofty lovely woman,"
    Says the lady in the furs,
In the glance she throws around her
    On the poorer dames and sirs:
"This robe, that cost three figures,
    Yes, is mine," her nod avers.

"True, my money did not buy it,
    But my husband's, from the trade;
And they, they only got it
    From things feeble and afraid
By murdering them in ambush
    With a cunning engine's aid.

"True, my hands, too, did not shape it
    To the pretty cut you see,
But the hands of midnight workers
    Who are strangers quite to me:
It was fitted, too, by dressers
    Ranged around me toilsomely.

"But I am a lovely lady,
    Though sneerers say I shine
By robbing Nature's children
    Of apparel not mine,
And that I am but a broom-stick,
    Like a scarecrow's wooden spine."

1925.

59

CHILDHOOD AMONG THE FERNS

I SAT one sprinkling day upon the lea,
    Where tall-stemmed ferns spread out
    luxuriantly,
And nothing but those tall ferns sheltered
    me.

The rain gained strength, and damped each
    lopping frond,
Ran down their stalks beside me and
    beyond,
And shaped slow-creeping rivulets as I
    conned,

With pride, my spray-roofed house. And
    though anon
Some drops pierced its green rafters, I
    sat on,
Making pretence I was not rained upon.

The sun then burst, and brought forth a
    sweet breath
From the limp ferns as they dried under-
    neath:
I said: "I could live on here thus till death";

CHILDHOOD AMONG THE FERNS

And queried in the green rays as I sate:
"Why should I have to grow to man's
    estate,
And this afar-noised World perambulate?"

A COUNTENANCE

HER laugh was not in the middle of her
    face quite,
  As a gay laugh springs,
It was plain she was anxious about some
    things
    I could not trace quite.
Her curls were like fir-cones — piled up,
    brown —
  Or rather like tight-tied sheaves:
It seemed they could never be taken
    down. . . .

And her lips were too full, some might say:
I did not think so. Anyway,
The shadow her lower one would cast
Was green in hue whenever she passed
    Bright sun on midsummer leaves.
Alas, I knew not much of her,
And lost all sight and touch of her!

If otherwise, should I have minded
The shy laugh not in the middle of her mouth
    quite,
And would my kisses have died of drouth
    quite
    As love became unblinded?
  1884.

A POET'S THOUGHT

IT sprang up out of him in the dark,
    And took on the lightness of a lark:
It went from his chamber along the city
    strand,
Lingered awhile, then leapt all over the
    land.

It came back maimed and mangled. And
    the poet
When he beheld his offspring did not know
    it:
Yea, verily, since its birth Time's tongue had
    tossed to him
Such travesties that his old thought was
    lost to him.

SILENCES

THERE is the silence of a copse or croft
      When the wind sinks dumb,
      And of a belfry-loft
When the tenor after tolling stops its hum.

And there's the silence of a lonely pond
      Where a man was drowned,
      Nor nigh nor yond
A newt, frog, toad, to make the merest sound.

But the rapt silence of an empty house
      Where oneself was born,
      Dwelt, held carouse
With friends, is of all silences most forlorn!

Past are remembered songs and music-
    strains
      Once audible there:
      Roof, rafters, panes
Look absent-thoughted, tranced, or locked
    in prayer.

It seems no power on earth can waken it
      Or rouse its rooms,
      Or its past permit
The present to stir a torpor like a tomb's.

"I WATCHED A BLACKBIRD"

I WATCHED a blackbird on a budding
   sycamore
One Easter Day, when sap was stirring twigs
      to the core;
   I saw his tongue, and crocus-coloured
      bill
   Parting and closing as he turned his trill;
   Then he flew down, seized on a stem of
      hay,
And upped to where his building scheme was
      under way,
As if so sure a nest were never shaped on
   spray.

A NIGHTMARE, AND THE
NEXT THING

ON this decline of Christmas Day
    The empty street is fogged and blurred:
The house-fronts all seem backwise turned
As if the outer world were spurned:
Voices and songs within are heard,
Whence red rays gleam when fires are
    stirred,
Upon this nightmare Christmas Day.

The lamps, just lit, begin to outloom
Like dandelion-globes in the gloom;
The stonework, shop-signs, doors, look
    bald;
Curious crude details seem installed,
And show themselves in their degrees
As they were personalities
Never discerned when the street was bus-
    tling
With vehicles, and farmers hustling.

Three clammy casuals wend their way
To the Union House.   I hear one say:
"Jimmy, this is a treat!   Hay-hay!"

A NIGHTMARE, AND THE NEXT THING

Six laughing mouths, six rows of teeth,
Six radiant pairs of eyes, beneath
Six yellow hats, looking out at the back
Of a waggonette on its slowed-down track
Up the steep street to some gay dance,
Suddenly interrupt my glance.

They do not see a gray nightmare
Astride the day, or anywhere.

TO A TREE IN LONDON

(CLEMENT'S INN)

H ERE you stay
    Night and day,
Never, never going away!

   Do you ache
   When we take
Holiday for our health's sake?

   Wish for feet
   When the heat
Scalds you in the brick-built street,

   That you might
   Climb the height
Where your ancestry saw light,

   Find a brook
   In some nook
There to purge your swarthy look?

   No.   You read
   Trees to need
Smoke like earth whereon to feed. . . .

68

TO A TREE IN LONDON

Have no sense
That far hence
Air is sweet in a blue immense,

Thus, black, blind,
You have opined
Nothing of your brightest kind;

Never seen
Miles of green,
Smelt the landscape's sweet serene.

192—.

THE FELLED ELM AND SHE

WHEN you put on that inmost ring
     She, like you, was a little thing:
When your circles reached their fourth,
Scarce she knew life's south from north:
When your year-zones counted twenty
She had fond admirers plenty:
When you'd grown your twenty-second
She and I were lovers reckoned:
When you numbered twenty-three
She went everywhere with me:
When you, at your fortieth line,
Showed decay, she seemed to pine:
When you were quite hollow within
She was felled — mere bone and skin:
You too, lacking strength to grow
Further trunk-rings, were laid low,
Matching her; both unaware
That your lives formed such a pair.

HE DID NOT KNOW ME

(Woman's Sorrow Song)

HE said : "I do not know you ;
You are not she who came
And made my heart grow tame?"
I laughed : "The same!"

Still said he : "I don't know you."
— "But I am your Love!" laughed I :
"Yours — faithful ever — till I die,
And pulseless lie!"

Yet he said : "I don't know you."
Freakful, I went away,
And met pale Time, with "Pray,
What means his Nay?"

Said Time : "He does not know you
In your mask of Comedy."
— "But," said I, "that I have chosen to be :
Tragedy he."

— "True ; hence he did not know you."
— "But him I could recognize?"
— "Yea.   Tragedy is true guise,
Comedy lies."

SO VARIOUS

YOU may have met a man — quite young —
A brisk-eyed youth, and highly strung:
  One whose desires
  And inner fires
  Moved him as wires.

And you may have met one stiff and old,
If not in years; of manner cold;
  Who seemed as stone,
  And never had known
  Of mirth or moan.

And there may have crossed your path a
  lover,
In whose clear depths you could discover
  A staunch, robust,
  And tender trust,
  Through storm and gust.

And you may have also known one fickle,
Whose fancies changed as the silver sickle
  Of yonder moon,
  Which shapes so soon
  To demilune!

SO VARIOUS

You entertained a person once
Whom you internally deemed a dunce : —
  As he sat in view
  Just facing you
  You saw him through.

You came to know a learned seer
Of whom you read the surface mere :
  Your soul quite sank ;
  Brain of such rank
  Dubbed yours a blank.

Anon you quizzed a man of sadness,
Who never could have known true gladness.
  Just for a whim
  You pitied him
  In his sore trim.

You journeyed with a man so glad
You never could conceive him sad :
  He proved to be
  Indubitably
  Good company.

You lit on an unadventurous slow man,
Who, said you, need be feared by no man ;
  That his slack deeds
  And sloth must needs
  Produce but weeds.

SO VARIOUS

A man of enterprise, shrewd and swift,
Who never suffered affairs to drift,
    You eyed for a time
    Just in his prime,
    And judged he might climb.

You smoked beside one who forgot
All that you said, or grasped it not.
    Quite a poor thing,
    Not worth a sting
    By satirizing!

Next year you nearly lost for ever
Goodwill from one who forgot slights never;
    And, with unease,
    Felt you must seize
    Occasion to please . . .

Now. . . . All these specimens of man,
So various in their pith and plan,
    Curious to say
    Were *one* man.   Yea,
    I was all they.

74

A SELF–GLAMOURER

MY little happiness,
  How much I have made of it!—
As if I had been not less
Than a queen, to be straight obeyed of it.
 "Life, be fairer far,"
  I said, "Than you are."

So I counted my springtime-day's
  Dream of futurity
Enringed with golden rays
To be quite a summer surety;
 And my trustful daring undoubt
  Brought it about!

Events all human-wrought
  Had look of divinity,
And what I foreframed in thought
Grew substanced, by force of affinity:
 Visions to verities came,
  Seen as the same.

My years in trusting spent
  Make to shape towardly,
And fate and accident
Behave not perversely or frowardly.
 Shall, then, Life's winter snow
  To me be so?

THE DEAD BASTARD

MANY and many a time I thought,
  "Would my child were in its grave!"
Such the trouble and shame it brought.

Now 'tis there.   And now I'd brave
Opinion's worst, in word or act,
To have that child alive; yes, slave

To dress and flaunt it to attract;
Show it the gossips brazenly,
And let as nothing be the fact
That never its father married me.

THE CLASPED SKELETONS

SURMISED DATE 1800 B.C.

*(In an ancient British barrow near the
writer's house)*

O WHY did we uncover to view
    So closely clasped a pair?
Your chalky bedclothes over you,
    This long time here!

Ere Paris lay with Helena —
    The poets' dearest Dear —
Ere David bedded Bathsheba
    You two were bedded here.

Aye, even before the beauteous Jael
    Bade Sisera doff his gear
And lie in her tent; then drove the nail,
    You two lay here.

Wicked Aholah, in her youth,
    Colled loves from far and near
Until they slew her without ruth;
    But you had long colled here.

Aspasia lay with Pericles,
    And Philip's son found cheer
At eves in lying on Thais' knees
    While you lay here.

77

THE CLASPED SKELETONS

Cleopatra with Antony,
  Resigned to dalliance sheer,
Lay, fatuous he, insatiate she,
  Long after you'd lain here.

Pilate by Procula his wife
  Lay tossing at her tear
Of pleading for an innocent life;
  You tossed not here.

Ages before Monk Abélard
  Gained tender Héloise' ear,
And loved and lay with her till scarred,
  Had you lain loving here.

So long, beyond chronology,
  Lovers in death as 'twere,
So long in placid dignity
  Have you lain here!

Yet what is length of time?   But dream!
  Once breathed this atmosphere
Those fossils near you, met the gleam
  Of day as you did here;

But so far earlier theirs beside
  Your life-span and career,
That they might style of yestertide
  Your coming here!

IN THE MARQUEE

IT was near last century's ending,
  And, though not much to rate
In a world of getting and spending,
  To her it was great.

The scene was a London suburb
  On a night of summer weather,
And the villas had back gardens
  Running together.

Her neighbours behind were dancing
  Under a marquee;
Two violoncellos played there,
  And violins three.

She had not been invited,
  Although her lover was;
She lay beside her husband,
  Perplexed at the cause.

Sweet after sweet quadrille rang:
  Absence made her weep;
The tears dried on her eyelids
  As she fell asleep.

79

IN THE MARQUEE

She dreamt she was whirling with him
 In this dance upon the green
To which she was not invited
  Though her lover had been.

All night she danced as he clasped her —
 That is, in the happy dream
The music kept her dreaming
  Till the first daybeam.

"O damn those noisy fiddles!"
 Her husband said as he turned:
"Close to a neighbour's bedroom:
  I'd like them burned!"

At intervals thus all night-long
 Her husband swore.   But she
Slept on, and danced in the loved arms,
  Under the marquee.

Next day she found that her lover,
 Though asked, had gone elsewhere,
And that she had possessed him in absence
  More than if there.

AFTER THE BURIAL

THE family had buried him,
   Their bread-bringer, their best :
They had returned to the house, whose hush
    a dim
   Vague vacancy expressed.

There sat his sons, mute, rigid-faced,
   His daughters, strained, red-eyed,
His wife, whose wan, worn features, vigil-
    traced,
   Bent over him when he died.

At once a peal bursts from the bells
   Of a large tall tower hard by :
Along the street the jocund clangour
    swells,
   And upward to the sky.

Probably it was a wedding-peal,
   Or possibly for a birth,
Or townsman knighted for political zeal,
   This resonant mark of mirth.

AFTER THE BURIAL

The mourners, heavy-browed, sat on
    Motionless.　Well they heard,
They　could　not　help　it；　nevertheless
    thereon
    Spoke not a single word,

Nor window did they close, to numb
    The bells' insistent calls
Of joy；　but suffered the harassing din to
    come
    And penetrate their souls.

THE MONGREL

IN Havenpool Harbour the ebb was
    strong,
And a man with a dog drew near and hung,
And taxpaying day was coming along,
    So the mongrel had to be drowned.
The man threw a stick from the paved
    wharf-side
Into the midst of the ebbing tide,
And the dog jumped after with ardent pride
    To bring the stick aground.

But no: the steady suck of the flood
To seaward needed, to be withstood,
More than the strength of mongrelhood
    To fight its treacherous trend.
So, swimming for life with desperate will,
The struggler with all his natant skill
Kept buoyant in front of his master, still
    There standing to wait the end.

The loving eyes of the dog inclined
To the man he held as a god enshrined,
With no suspicion in his mind
    That this had all been meant.

83

THE MONGREL

Till the effort not to drift from shore
Of his little legs grew slower and slower,
And, the tide still outing with brookless
    power,
      Outward the dog, too, went.

Just ere his sinking what does one see
Break on the face of that devotee?
A wakening to the treachery
      He had loved with love so blind?
The faith that had shone in that mongrel's
    eye
That his owner would save him by and by
Turned to much like a curse as he sank to
    die,
      And a loathing of mankind.

CONCERNING AGNES

I AM stopped from hoping what I have
hoped before —
　　Yes, many a time! —
　To dance with that fair woman yet once
more
　　As in the prime
　Of August, when the wide-faced moon
looked through
The boughs at the faery lamps of the Larmer
Avenue.

　I could not, though I should wish, have
over again
　　That old romance,
　And sit apart in the shade as we sat then
　　After the dance
　The while I held her hand, and, to the
booms
Of contrabassos, feet still pulsed from the
distant rooms.

　I could not. And you do not ask me
why.
　　Hence you infer

CONCERNING AGNES

That what may chance to the fairest
    under the sky
        Has chanced to her.
Yes. She lies white, straight, features
    marble-keen,
Unapproachable, mute, in a nook I have
    never seen.

There she may rest like some vague
    goddess, shaped
        As out of snow ;
Say Aphrodite sleeping ; or bedraped
        Like Kalupso ;
Or Amphitrite stretched on the Mid-sea
    swell,
Or one of the Nine grown stiff from thought.
    I cannot tell !

HENLEY REGATTA

SHE looks from the window: still it pours
     down direly,
And the avenue drips. She cannot go, she
     fears;
And the Regatta will be spoilt entirely;
     And she sheds half-crazed tears.

Regatta Day and rain come on together
Again, years after. Gutters trickle loud;
But Nancy cares not. She knows nought
     of weather,
     Or of the Henley crowd:

She's a Regatta quite her own. Inanely
She laughs in the asylum as she floats
Within a water-tub, which she calls
     "Henley,"
     Her little paper boats.

AN EVENING IN GALILEE

SHE looks far west towards Carmel,
　　shading her eyes with her hand,
And she then looks east to the Jordan, and
　　the smooth Tiberias' strand.
"Is my son mad?" she asks; and never
　　an answer has she,
Save from herself, aghast at the possibility.
"He professes as his firm faiths things far
　　too grotesque to be true,
And his vesture is odd — too careless for
　　one of his fair young hue! . . .

"He lays down doctrines as if he were old
　　— aye, fifty at least:
In the Temple he terrified me, opposing
　　the very High-Priest!
Why did he say to me, 'Woman, what have
　　I to do with thee?'
O it cuts to the heart that a child of mine
　　thus spoke to me!
And he said, too, 'Who is my mother?' —
　　when he knows so very well.
He might have said, 'Who is my father?'
　　— and I'd found it hard to tell!

That no one knows but Joseph and — one
    other, nor ever will;
One who'll not see me again. . . . How it
    chanced! — I dreaming no ill! . . .

"Would he'd not mix with the lowest folk
    — like those fishermen —
The while so capable, culling new knowl-
    edge, beyond our ken! . . .
That woman of no good character, ever
    following him,
Adores him if I mistake not: his wish of
    her is but a whim
Of his madness, it may be, outmarking his
    lack of coherency;
After his 'Keep the Commandments!' to
    smile upon such as she!
It is just what all those do who are wander-
    ing in their wit.
I don't know — dare not say — what harm
    may grow from it.
O a mad son is a terrible thing; it even may
    lead
To arrest, and death! . . . And how he
    can preach, expound, and read!

"Here comes my husband. Shall I unveil
    him this tragedy-brink?

No.   He has nightmares enough.   I'll pray,
    and think, and think." . . .
She remembers she's never put on any pot
    for his evening meal,
And pondering a plea looks vaguely to
    south of her — towards Jezreel.

THE BROTHER

O KNOW you what I have done
   To avenge our sister? She,
I thought, was wantoned with
By a man of levity:

And I lay in wait all day,
All day did I wait for him,
And dogged him to Bollard Head
When twilight dwindled dim,

And hurled him over the edge
And heard him fall below:
O would I were lying with him,
For the truth I did not know!

"O where's my husband?" she asked,
As evening wore away:
"Best you had one, forsooth,
But never had you!" I say.

"Yes, but I have!" says she,
"My Love made it up with me,
And we churched it yesterday
And mean to live happily."

THE BROTHER

And now I go in haste
To the Head, before she's aware,
To join him in death for the wrong
I've done them both out there!

WE FIELD–WOMEN

How it rained
    When we worked at Flint-
        comb-Ash,
And could not stand upon the hill
Trimming swedes for the slicing-mill.
The wet washed through us — plash, plash,
    plash :
        How it rained !

        How it snowed
When we crossed from Flintcomb-Ash
To the Great Barn for drawing reed,
Since we could nowise chop a swede. —
Flakes in each doorway and casement-sash :
        How it snowed !

        How it shone
When we went from Flintcomb-Ash
To start at dairywork once more
In the laughing meads, with cows three-
    score,
And pails, and songs, and love — too rash :
        How it shone !

A PRACTICAL WOMAN

"O WHO'LL get me a healthy child : —
    I should prefer a son —
Seven have I had in thirteen years,
    Sickly every one!

"Three mope about as feeble shapes;
    Weak; white; they'll be no good.
One came deformed; an idiot next;
    And two are crass as wood.

"I purpose one not only sound
    In flesh, but bright in mind:
And duly for producing him
    A means I've now to find."

She went away. She disappeared,
    Years, years. Then back she came:
In her hand was a blooming boy
    Mentally and in frame.

"I found a father at last who'd suit
    The purpose in my head,
And used him till he'd done his job,"
    Was all thereon she said.

SQUIRE HOOPER

HOOPER was ninety. One September dawn
    He sent a messenger
For his physician, who asked thereupon
    What ailed the sufferer
Which he might circumvent, and promptly
    bid begone.

"Doctor, I summoned you," the squire
    replied —
    "Pooh-pooh me though you may —
To ask what's happened to me — burst
    inside,
    It seems — not much, I'd say —
But awkward with a house-full here for a
    shoot to-day."

And he described the symptoms. With
    bent head
    The listener looked grave.
"H'm. . . . *You're a dead man in six
    hours*," he said. —
    "I speak out, since you are brave —
And best 'tis you should know, that last
    things may be sped."

SQUIRE HOOPER

"Right," said the squire. "And now
     comes — what to do?
  One thing: on no account
Must I now spoil the sport I've asked
     them to —
  My guests are paramount —
They must scour scrub and stubble; and
     big bags bring as due."

He downed to breakfast, and bespoke
     his guests: —
  "I find I have to go
An unexpected journey, and it rests
  With you, my friends, to show
The shoot can go off gaily, whether I'm
     there or no."

Thus blandly spoke he; and to the fields
     they went,
  And Hooper up the stair.
They had a glorious day; and stiff and
     spent
  Returned as dusk drew near. —
"Gentlemen," said the doctor, "he's not back
     as meant,

To his deep regret!" — So they took
     leave, each guest
  Observing: "I dare say
96

SQUIRE HOOPER

Business detains him in the town: 'tis
    best
  We should no longer stay
Just now. We'll come again anon ;" and
    they went their way.

  Meeting two men in the obscurity
    Shouldering a box a thin
Cloth-covering wrapt, one sportsman
    cried : "Damn me,
  I thought them carrying in,
At first, a coffin ; till I knew it could not
    be."

"A GENTLEMAN'S SECOND–HAND SUIT"

HERE it is hanging in the sun
        By the pawn-shop door,
A dress-suit — all its revels done
        Of heretofore.
Long drilled to the waltzers' swing and sway,
        As its tokens show:
What it has seen, what it could say
        If it did but know!

The sleeve bears still a print of powder
        Rubbed from her arms
When she warmed up as the notes swelled
        louder
        And livened her charms —
Or rather theirs, for beauties many
        Leant there, no doubt,
Leaving these tell-tale traces when he
        Spun them about.

Its cut seems rather in bygone style
        On looking close,
So it mayn't have bent it for some while
        To the dancing pose:

98

"A GENTLEMAN'S SECOND-HAND SUIT"

Anyhow, often within its clasp
        Fair partners hung,
Assenting to the wearer's grasp
        With soft sweet tongue.

Where is, alas, the gentleman
        Who wore this suit?
And where are his ladies?   Tell none can:
        Gossip is mute.
Some of them may forget him quite
        Who smudged his sleeve,
Some think of a wild and whirling night
        With him, and grieve.

"WE SAY WE SHALL NOT MEET"

WE say we shall not meet
    Again beneath this sky,
And turn with leaden feet,
    Murmuring "Good-bye!"

But laugh at how we rued
Our former time's adieu
When those who went for good
    Are met anew.

We talk in lightest vein
On trifles talked before,
And part to meet again,
    But meet no more.

SEEING THE MOON RISE

WE used to go to Froom-hill Barrow
    To see the round moon rise
    Into the heath-rimmed skies,
Trudging thither by plough and harrow
Up the pathway, steep and narrow,
    Singing a song.
Now we do not go there.   Why?
    Zest burns not so high!

Latterly we've only conned her
    With a passing glance
    From window or door by chance,
Hoping to go again, high yonder,
As we used, and gaze, and ponder,
    Singing a song.
Thitherward we do not go:
    Feet once quick are slow!

August 1927.

SONG TO AURORE

WE'LL not begin again to love,
    It only leads to pain;
The fire we now are master of
    Has seared us not in vain.
Any new step of yours I'm fain
    To hear of from afar,
And even in such may find a gain
    While lodged not where you are.

No : that must not be done anew
    Which has been done before;
I scarce could bear to seek, or view,
    Or clasp you any more!
Life is a labour, death is sore,
    And lonely living wrings;
But go your courses, sweet Aurore,
    Kisses are caresome things!

HE NEVER EXPECTED MUCH

[or]

A CONSIDERATION

[*A reflection*] ON MY EIGHTY-SIXTH BIRTHDAY

WELL, World, you have kept faith with
      me,
    Kept faith with me;
Upon the whole you have proved to be
    Much as you said you were.
Since as a child I used to lie
Upon the leaze and watch the sky,
Never, I own, expected I
    That life would all be fair.

'Twas then you said, and since have said,
    Times since have said,
In that mysterious voice you shed
    From clouds and hills around:
"Many have loved me desperately,
Many with smooth serenity,
While some have shown contempt of me
    Till they dropped underground.

HE NEVER EXPECTED MUCH

"I do not promise overmuch,
      Child ; overmuch ;
Just neutral-tinted haps and such,"
      You said to minds like mine.
Wise warning for your credit's sake !
Which I for one failed not to take,
And hence could stem such strain and ache
      As each year might assign.

STANDING BY THE
MANTELPIECE

(H. M. M., 1873)

THIS candle-wax is shaping to a shroud
    To-night. (They call it that, as you
    may know) —
By touching it the claimant is avowed,
And hence I press it with my finger — so.

To-night. To me twice night, that should
    have been
The radiance of the midmost tick of noon,
And close around me wintertime is seen
That might have shone the veriest day of
    June!

But since all's lost, and nothing really lies
Above but shade, and shadier shade below,
Let me make clear, before one of us dies,
My mind to yours, just now embittered so.

Since you agreed, unurged and full-advised,
And let warmth grow without discourage-
    ment,

STANDING BY THE MANTELPIECE

Why do you bear you now as if surprised,
When what has come was clearly con-
     sequent?

Since you have spoken, and finality
Closes around, and my last movements
     loom,
I say no more: the rest must wait till we
Are face to face again, yonside the tomb.

And let the candle-wax thus mould a shape
Whose meaning now, if hid before, you
     know,
And how by touch one present claims its
     drape,
And that it's I who press my finger — so.

BOYS THEN AND NOW

"MORE than one cuckoo?"
   And the little boy
Seemed to lose something
Of his spring joy.

When he'd grown up
He told his son
He'd used to think
There was only one,

Who came each year
With the trees' new trim
On purpose to please
England and him:

And his son — old already
In life and its ways —
Said yawning: "How foolish
Boys were in those days!"

THAT KISS IN THE DARK

RECALL it you? —
     Say you do! —
When you went out into the night,
In an impatience that would not wait,
From that lone house in the woodland spot,
And when I, thinking you had gone
For ever and ever from my sight,
Came after, printing a kiss upon
        Black air
        In my despair,
And my two lips lit on your cheek
As you leant silent against a gate,
Making my woman's face flush hot
At what I had done in the dark, unware
You lingered for me but would not speak:
Yes, kissed you, thinking you were not
    there!
        Recall it you? —
        Say you do!

A NECESSITARIAN'S EPITAPH

A WORLD I did not wish to enter
    Took me and poised me on my centre,
Made me grimace, and foot, and prance,
As cats on hot bricks have to dance
Strange jigs to keep them from the floor,
Till they sink down and feel no more.

BURNING THE HOLLY

O YOU are sad on Twelfth Night,
   I notice: sad on Twelfth Night;
You are as sad on Twelfth Night
      As any that I know.

"Yes: I am sad on that night,
Doubtless I'm sad on that night:
Yes; I am sad on that night,
      For we all loved her so!"

Why are you sad on Twelfth Night,
Especially on Twelfth Night?
Why are you sad on Twelfth Night
      When wit and laughter flow?

— "She'd been a famous dancer,
Much lured of men; a dancer.
She'd been a famous dancer,
      Facile in heel and toe. . . .

"And we were burning the holly
On Twelfth Night; the holly,
As people do: the holly,
      Ivy, and mistletoe.

BURNING THE HOLLY

"And while it popped and crackled,
(She being our lodger), crackled;
And while it popped and crackled,
    Her face caught by the glow,

"In he walked and said to her,
In a slow voice he said to her;
Yes, walking in he said to her,
    'We sail before cock-crow.'

"'Why did you not come on to me,
As promised? Yes, come on to me?
Why did you not come on to me,
    Since you had sworn to go?'

"His eyes were deep and flashing,
As flashed the holm-flames: flashing;
His eyes were deep, and flashing
    In their quick, keen upthrow.

"As if she had been ready,
Had furtively been ready;
As if she had been ready
    For his insistence — lo! —

"She clasped his arm and went with him
As his entirely: went with him.
She clasped his arm and went with him
    Into the sprinkling snow.

BURNING THE HOLLY

"We saw the prickly leaves waste
To ashes : saw the leaves waste ;
The burnt-up prickly leaves waste. . . .
    The pair had gone also.

— "On Twelfth Night, two years after —
Yes, Twelfth Night, two years after ;
On Twelfth Night, two years after,
    We sat — our spirits low —

"Musing, when back the door swung
Without a knock.   The door swung ;
Thought flew to her.   The door swung,
    And in she came, pale, slow ;

"Against her breast a child clasped ;
Close to her breast a child clasped ;
She stood there with the child clasped,
    Swaying it to and fro.

"Her look alone the tale told ;
Quite wordless was the tale told ;
Her careworn eyes the tale told
    As larger they seemed to grow. . . .

"One day next spring she disappeared,
The second time she disappeared.
And that time, when she'd disappeared
    Came back no more.   Ah, no !

BURNING THE HOLLY

"But we still burn the holly
On Twelfth Night; burn the holly
As people do: the holly,
    Ivy, and mistletoe."

SUSPENSE

A CLAMMINESS hangs over all like a
clout,
The fields are a water-colour washed out,
The sky at its rim leaves a chink of light,
Like the lid of a pot that will not close tight.

She is away by the groaning sea,
Strained at the heart, and waiting for me :
Between us our foe from a hid retreat
Is watching, to wither us if we meet. . . .

But it matters little, however we fare —
Whether we meet, or I get not there ;
The sky will look the same thereupon,
And the wind and the sea go groaning on.

THE SECOND VISIT

CLACK, clack, clack, went the mill-wheel
    as I came,
And she was on the bridge with the thin
    hand-rail,
And the miller at the door, and the ducks
    at mill-tail ;
I come again years after, and all there seems
    the same.

And so indeed it is : the apple-tree'd old
    house,
And the deep mill pond, and the wet wheel
    clacking,
And a woman on the bridge, and white
    ducks quacking,
And the miller at the door, powdered pale
    from boots to brows.

But it's not the same miller whom long ago
    I knew,
Nor are they the same apples, nor the same
    drops that dash
Over the wet wheel, nor the ducks below
    that splash,
Nor the woman who to fond plaints replied,
    "You know I do !"

OUR OLD FRIEND DUALISM

ALL hail to him, the Protean! A tough
    old chap is he:
Spinoza and the Monists cannot make him
    cease to be.
We pound him with our "Truth, Sir, please!"
    and quite appear to still him:
He laughs; holds Bergson up, and James;
    and swears we cannot kill him.
We argue them pragmatic cheats. "Aye,"
    says he. "They're deceiving:
But I must live; for flamens plead I am all
    that's worth believing!"

1920.

FAITHFUL WILSON

"I SAY she's handsome, by all laws
  Of beauty, if wife ever was!"
Wilson insists thus, though each day
The years fret Fanny towards decay.
"She *was* once beauteous as a jewel,"
Hint friends; "but Time, of course, is cruel."
Still Wilson does not quite feel how,
Once fair, she can be different now.

Partly from Strato of Sardis.

GALLANT'S SONG

WHEN the maiden leaves off teasing,
   Then the man may leave off pleasing:
      Yea, 'tis sign,
      Wet or fine,
She will love him without ceasing
With a love there's no appeasing.
      Is it so?
      Ha-ha.   Ho!

Nov. 1868.
   From an old notebook.

A PHILOSOPHICAL FANTASY

"Milton . . . made God argue." — WALTER BAGEHOT.

"WELL, if thou wilt, then, ask me;
　　　To answer will not task me:
I've a response, I doubt not,
And quite agree to flout not
Thy question, if of reason,
Albeit not quite in season:
A universe to marshal,
What god can give but partial
Eye to frail Earth — life-shotten
Ere long, extinct, forgotten! —
But seeing indications
That thou read'st my limitations,
And since my lack of forethought
Aggrieves thy more and more thought,
I'll hearken to thy pleading:
Some lore may lie in heeding
Thy irregular proceeding."

"'Tis this *unfulfilled intention*,
O Causer, I would mention: —
Will you, in condescension
This evening, ere we've parted,
Say why you felt fainthearted,

A PHILOSOPHICAL FANTASY

And let your aim be thwarted,
Its glory be diminished,
Its concept stand unfinished? —
Such I ask you, Sir or Madam,
(I know no more than Adam,
Even vaguely, what your sex is, —
Though feminine I had thought you
Till seers as 'Sire' besought you ; —
And this my ignorance vexes
Some people not a little,
And, though not me one tittle,
It makes me sometimes choose me
Call you 'It,' if you'll excuse me?")

"Call me 'It' with a good conscience,
And be sure it is all nonsense
That I mind a fault of manner
In a pigmy towards his planner !
Be I, be not I, sexless,
I am in nature vexless.
— How vain must clay-carved man be
To deem such folly can be
As that freaks of my own framing
Can set my visage flaming —
Start me volleying interjections
Against my own confections,
As the Jews and others limned me,
And in fear and trembling hymned me !

A PHILOSOPHICAL FANTASY

Call me 'but dream-projected,'
I shall not be affected ;
Call me 'blind force persisting,'
I shall remain unlisting ;
(A few have done it lately,
And, maybe, err not greatly.)
— Another such a vanity
In witless weak humanity
Is thinking that of those all
Through space at my disposal,
Man's shape must needs resemble
Mine, that makes zodiacs tremble !

"Continuing where we started : —
As for my aims being thwarted,
Wherefore I feel fainthearted,
Aimless am I, revealing
No heart-scope for faint feeling.
— But thy mistake I'll pardon,
And, as Adam's mentioned to me,
(Though in timeless truth there never
Was a man like him whatever,)
I'll meet thee in thy garden,
As I did not him, beshrew me !
In the sun of so-called daytime —
Say, just about the Maytime
Of my next, or next, Creation ?
(I love procrastination,

To use the words in thy sense,
Which have no hold on my sense)
Or at any future stray-time —
One of thy representatives
In some later incarnation
I mean, of course, well knowing
Thy present conformation
But a unit of my tentatives,
Whereof such heaps lie blowing
As dust, where thou art going;
Yea, passed to where suns glow not,
Begrieved of those that go not,
(Though what grief is, I know not.)

"Perhaps I may inform thee,
In case I should alarm thee,
That no dramatic stories
Like ancient ones whose core is
A mass of superstition
And monkish imposition
Will mark my explanation
Of the world's sore situation
(As thou tell'st), with woes that shatter;
Though from former aions to latter
To me 'tis malleable matter
For treatment scientific
More than sensitive and specific —
Stuff without moral features,

A PHILOSOPHICAL FANTASY

Which I've no sense of ever,
Or of ethical endeavour,
Or of justice to Earth's creatures,
Or how Right from Wrong to sever:
Let these be as men learn such;
For me, I don't discern such,
And — real enough I daresay —
I know them but by hearsay
As something Time hath rendered
Out of substance I engendered,
Time, too, being a condition
Beyond my recognition.
— I would add that, while unknowing
Of this justice earthward owing,
Nor explanation offering
Of what is meant by suffering,
Thereof I'm not a spurner,
Or averse to be a learner.

"To return from wordy wandering
To the question we are pondering;
Though, viewing the world in *my* mode,
I fail to see it in *thy* mode
As 'unfulfilled intention,'
Which is past my comprehension
Being unconscious in my doings
So largely, (whence thy rueings); —
Aye, to human tribes nor kindlessness

A PHILOSOPHICAL FANTASY

Nor love I've given, but mindlessness,
Which state, though far from ending,
May nevertheless be mending.

"However, I'll advise him —
Him thy scion, who will walk here
When Death hath dumbed thy talk here —
In phrase that may surprise him,
What thing it was befel me,
(A thing that my confessing
Lack of forethought helps thy guessing),
And acted to compel me
By that *purposeless propension*
Which is mine, and not intention,
Along lines of least resistance,
Or, in brief, unsensed persistence,
That saddens thy existence
To think my so-called scheming
Not that of my first dreaming."

1920 and 1926.

A QUESTION OF MARRIAGE

"I YIELD you my whole heart, Coun-
    tess," said he ;
"Come, Dear, and be queen of my studio."
"No, sculptor. You're merely my friend,"
    said she :
"We dine our artists ; but marry them —
    no."

"Be it thus," he replied. And his love,
    so strong,
He subdued as a stoic should. Anon
He wived some damsel who'd loved him long,
Of lineage noteless ; and chiselled on.

And a score years passed. As a master-
    mind
The world made much of his marching
    fame,
And his wife's little charms, with his own
    entwined,
Won day after day increased acclaim.

The countess-widow had closed with a mate
In rank and wealth of her own degree,

And they moved among the obscurely
    great
Of an order that had no novelty.

And oldening — neither with blame nor
    praise —
Their stately lives begot no stir,
And she saw that when death should efface
    her days
All men would abandon thought of her;

And said to herself full gloomily:
"Far better for me had it been to shine
The wench of a genius such as he
Than rust as the wife of a spouse like
    mine!"

THE LETTER'S TRIUMPH

(A FANCY)

YES: I perceive it's to your Love
   You are bent on sending me.
      That this is so
      Your words and phrases prove!

And now I am folded, and start to go,
Where you, my writer, have no leave to
         come:
      My entry none will know!

And I shall catch her eye, and dumb
She'll keep, should my unnoised arrival be
      Hoped for, or troublesome.

My face she'll notice readily:
And, whether she care to meet you, or care
         not,
      She will perforce meet me;

Take me to closet or garden-plot
And, blushing or pouting, bend her eyes
         quite near,
      Moved much, or never a jot.

THE LETTER'S TRIUMPH

And while you wait in hope and fear,
Far from her cheeks and lips, snug I shall
stay
In close communion there,

And hear her heart-beats, things she
may say,
As near her naked fingers, sleeve, or glove
I lie — ha-ha! — all day.

A FORGOTTEN MINIATURE

THERE you are in the dark,
    Deep in a box
Nobody ever unlocks,
Or even turns to mark;
    — Out of mind stark.

Yet there you have not been worsed
    Like your sitter
By Time, the Fair's hard-hitter;
Your beauties, undispersed,
    Glow as at first.

Shut in your case for years,
    Never an eye
Of the many passing nigh,
Fixed on their own affairs,
    Thinks what it nears!

— While you have lain in gloom,
    A form forgot,
Your reign remembered not,
Much life has come to bloom
    Within this room.

A FORGOTTEN MINIATURE

Yea, in Time's cyclic sweep
    Unrest has ranged :
Women and men have changed :
Some you knew slumber deep ;
    Some wait for sleep.

WHISPERED AT THE CHURCH–OPENING

IN the bran-new pulpit the bishop stands,
  And gives out his text, as his gaze expands
  To the people, the aisles, the roof's new frame,
  And the arches, and ashlar with coloured bands.

"Why — he's the man," says one, "who came
  To preach in my boyhood — a fashion then —
In a series of sermons to working-men
On week-day evenings, a novelty
Which brought better folk to hear and see.
They preached each one each week, by request:
Some were eloquent speakers, among the best
Of the lot being this, as all confessed."

"I remember now. And reflection brings
Back one in especial, sincerest of all;

Whose words, though unpicked, gave the
      essence of things ; —
And where is he now, whom I well recall?"

"Oh, he'd no touches of tactic skill :
His mind ran on charity and good will :
He's but as he was, a vicar still."

IN WEATHERBURY STOCKS

(1850)

"I SIT here in these stocks,
    And Saint-Mary's moans eleven;
The sky is dark and cold:
I would I were in heaven!

"What footsteps do I hear?
Ah, you do not forget,
My Sophy! O, my dear,
We may be happy yet!

"But —. Mother, is't your voice?
You who have come to me? —
It did not cross my thought:
I was thinking it was she."

"She! Foolish simple son!
She says: 'I've finished quite
With him or any one
Put in the stocks to-night.'

"She's gone to Blooms-End dance,
And will not come back yet:
Her new man sees his chance,
And is teaching her to forget.

133

"Jim, think no other woman
To such a fellow is true
But the mother you have grieved so,
Or cares for one like you!"

A PLACID MAN'S EPITAPH

AS for my life, I've led it
    With fair content and credit:
It said: "Take this." I took it.
Said: "Leave." And I forsook it.
If I had done without it
None would have cared about it,
Or said: "One has refused it
Who might have meetly used it."

1925.

THE NEW BOOTS

"THEY are his new boots," she pur-
  sued;
"They have not been worn at all:
They stay there hung on the wall,
And are getting as stiff as wood.
He bought them for the wet weather,
And they are of waterproof leather."

"Why does her husband," said I,
"Never wear those boots bought new?"
To a neighbour of hers I knew;
Who answered: "Ah, those boots. Aye,
He bought them to wear whenever
It rained. But there they hang ever.

"'Yes,' he laughed, as he hung them up,
'I've got them at last — a pair
I can walk in anywhere
Through rain and slush and slop.
For many a year I've been haunted
By thoughts of how much they were wanted.'

"And she's not touched them or tried
To remove them. . . . Anyhow,

THE NEW BOOTS

As you see them hanging now
They have hung ever since he died
The day after gaily declaring:
'Ha-ha! Now for wet wayfaring.
They're just the chaps for my wearing!'"

THE MUSING MAIDEN

"WHY so often, silent one,
    Do you steal away alone?"
Starting, half she turned her head,
  And guiltily she said:—

"When the vane points to his far town
I go upon the hog-backed down,
And think the breeze that stroked his lip
  Over my own may slip.

"When he walks at close of day
I ramble on the white highway,
And think it reaches to his feet:
  A meditation sweet!

"When coasters hence to London sail
I watch their puffed wings waning pale;
His window opens near the quay;
  Their coming he can see.

"I go to meet the moon at night;
To mark the moon was our delight;
Up there our eyesights touched at will
  If such he practise still."

W.P.V.
October 1866 (recopied).

138

LORNA THE SECOND

LORNA! Yes, you are sweet,
    But you are not your mother,
Lorna the First, frank, feat,
Never such another! —
Love of her could smother
Griefs by day or night;
Nor could any other,
Lorna, dear and bright,
Ever so well adorn a
Mansion, coach, or cot,
Or so make men scorn a
Rival in their sight;
Even you could not!
Hence I have to mourn a
Loss ere you were born; a
    Lorna!

A DAUGHTER RETURNS

I LIKE not that dainty-cut raiment, those
    earrings of pearl,
  I like not the light in that eye;
I like not the note of that voice. Never so
    was the girl
  Who a year ago bade me good-bye!

Hadst but come bare and moneyless, worn
    in the vamp, weather-gray,
  But innocent still as before,
How warmly I'd lodged thee! But sport
    thy new gains far away;
  I pray thee now — come here no more!

And yet I'll not try to blot out every memory
    of thee;
  I'll think of thee — yes, now and then:
One who's watched thee since Time called
    thee out o' thy mother and me
  Must think of thee; aye, I know when! . . .

When the cold sneer of dawn follows night-
    shadows black as a hearse,
  And the rain filters down the fruit tree,
And the tempest mouths into the flue-top
    a word like a curse,
  Then, then I shall think, think of thee!

Dec. 17, 1901.

THE THIRD KISSING–GATE

SHE foots it forward down the town,
    Then leaves the lamps behind,
And trots along the eastern road
    Where elms stand double-lined.

She clacks the first dim kissing-gate
    Beneath the storm-strained trees,
And passes to the second mead
    That fringes Mellstock Leaze.

She swings the second kissing-gate
    Next the gray garden-wall,
And sees the third mead stretching down
    Towards the waterfall.

And now the third-placed kissing-gate
    Her silent shadow nears,
And touches with; when suddenly
    Her person disappears.

What chanced by that third kissing-gate
    When the hushed mead grew dun?
Lo — two dark figures clasped and closed
    As if they were but one.

DRINKING SONG

ONCE on a time when thought began
    Lived Thales: he
    Was said to see
Vast truths that mortals seldom can;
    It seems without
    A moment's doubt
That everything was made for man.

Chorus

  Fill full your cups: feel no distress
  That thoughts so great should now be
    less!

Earth mid the sky stood firm and flat,
    He held, till came
    A sage by name
Copernicus, and righted that.
    We trod, he told,
    A globe that rolled
Around a sun it warmed it at.

Chorus

  Fill full your cups: feel no distress;
  'Tis only one great thought the less!

DRINKING SONG

But still we held, as Time flew by
  And wit increased,
  Ours was, at least,
The only world whose rank was high :
  Till rumours flew
  From folk who knew
Of globes galore about the sky.

Chorus

 Fill full your cups : feel no distress ;
 'Tis only one great thought the less !

And that this earth, our one estate,
  Was no prime ball,
  The best of all,
But common, mean ; indeed, tenth-rate :
  And men, so proud,
  A feeble crowd,
Unworthy any special fate.

Chorus

 Fill full your cups : feel no distress ;
 'Tis only one great thought the less !

Then rose one Hume, who could not see,
  If earth were such,
  Required were much

143

DRINKING SONG

To prove no miracles could be:
    "Better believe
    The eyes deceive
Than that God's clockwork jolts," said he.

Chorus

  Fill full your cups: feel no distress;
  'Tis only one great thought the less!

Next this strange message Darwin brings,
    (Though saying his say
    In a quiet way);
We all are one with creeping things;
    And apes and men
    Blood-brethren,
And likewise reptile forms with stings.

Chorus

  Fill full your cups: feel no distress;
  'Tis only one great thought the less!

And when this philosoph had done
    Came Doctor Cheyne:
    Speaking plain he
Proved no virgin bore a son.
    "Such tale, indeed,
    Helps not our creed,"
He said. "A tale long known to none."

DRINKING SONG

Chorus

Fill full your cups : feel no distress ;
'Tis only one great thought the less !

And now comes Einstein with a notion —
    Not yet quite clear
    To many here —
That's there's no time, no space, no motion,
    Nor rathe nor late,
    Nor square nor straight,
But just a sort of bending-ocean.

Chorus

Fill full your cups : feel no distress ;
'Tis only one great thought the less !

So here we are, in piteous case :
    Like butterflies
    Of many dyes
Upon an Alpine glacier's face :
    To fly and cower
    In some warm bower
Our chief concern in such a place.

Chorus

Fill full your cups : feel no distress
At all our great thoughts shrinking less :
We'll do a good deed nevertheless !

145

THE TARRYING BRIDEGROOM

WILDLY bound the bells this morning
For the glad solemnity;
People are adorning
Chancel and canopy;
But amid the peal a warning
Under-echo calls to me.

Where the lane divides the pasture
Long I watch each bend and stone,
Why not now as last year,
When he sought me — lone?
Come, O come, and see, and cast here
Light and love on one your own!

How it used to draw him to me,
When I piped a pretty tune;
Yes, when first he knew me
In my pink shalloon:
Little I guessed 'twould so undo me
Lacking him this summer noon!

THE DESTINED PAIR

TWO beings were drifting
  Each one to the other :
No moment's veil-lifting
Or hint from another
      Led either to weet
      That the tracks of their feet
      Were arcs that would meet.

One moved in a city,
And one in a village,
Where many a ditty
He tongued when at tillage
      On dreams of a dim
      Figure fancy would limn
      That was viewless to him.

Would Fate have been kinder
To keep night between them ? —
Had he failed to find her
And time never seen them
      Unite ; so that, caught
      In no burning love-thought,
      She had faded unsought ?

147

A MUSICAL INCIDENT

WHEN I see the room it hurts me
     As with a pricking blade,
Those women being the memoried reason
     why my cheer deserts me. —
     'Twas thus.   One of them played
     To please her friend, not knowing
     That friend was speedily growing,
     Behind the player's chair,
     Somnolent, unaware
     Of any music there.

I saw it, and it distressed me,
     For I had begun to think
I loved the drowsy listener, when this arose
          to test me
     And tug me from love's brink.
     "Beautiful!" said she, waking
     As the music ceased.   "Heartaching!"
     Though never a note she'd heard
     To judge of as averred —
     Save that of the very last word.

All would have faded in me,
     But that the sleeper brought

A MUSICAL INCIDENT

News a week thence that her friend was
       dead. It stirred within me
   Sense of injustice wrought
   That dead player's poor intent —
   So heartily, kindly meant —
   As blandly added the sigher:
   "How glad I am I was nigh her,
   To hear her last tune!" — "Liar!"
   I lipped. — This gave love pause,
   And killed it, such as it was.

JUNE LEAVES AND AUTUMN

I

LUSH summer lit the trees to green;
   But in the ditch hard by
Lay dying boughs some hand unseen
Had lopped when first with festal mien
   They matched their mates on high.
It seemed a melancholy fate
That leaves but brought to birth so late
   Should rust there, red and numb,
In quickened fall, while all their race
Still joyed aloft in pride of place
   With store of days to come.

II

At autumn-end I fared that way,
   And traced those boughs fore-hewn
Whose leaves, awaiting their decay
In slowly browning shades, still lay
   Where they had lain in June
And now, no less embrowned and curst
Than if they had fallen with the first,
   Nor known a morning more,
Lay there alongside, dun and sere,
Those that at my last wandering here
   Had length of days in store.

   Nov. 19, 1898.

NO BELL–RINGING

A BALLAD OF DURNOVER

THE little boy legged on through the
    dark,
  To hear the New-Year's ringing :
The three-mile road was empty, stark,
  No sound or echo bringing.

When he got to the tall church tower
  Standing upon the hill,
Although it was hard on the midnight hour
  The place was, as elsewhere, still ;

Except that the flag-staff rope, betossed
  By blasts from the nor'-east,
Like a dead man's bones on a gibbet-post
  Tugged as to be released.

"Why is there no ringing to-night?"
  Said the boy to a moveless one
On a tombstone where the moon struck
    white ;
  But he got answer none.

NO BELL-RINGING

"No ringing in of New Year's Day."
  He mused as he dragged back home;
And wondered till his head was gray
  Why the bells that night were dumb.

And often thought of the snowy shape
  That sat on the moonlit stone,
Nor spoke nor moved, and in mien and
      drape
  Seemed like a sprite thereon.

And then he met one left of the band
  That had treble-bobbed when young,
And said : "I never could understand
  Why, that night, no bells rung."

"True.   There'd not happened such a
      thing
  For half a century; aye,
And never I've told why they did not ring
  From that time till to-day. . . .

"Through the week in bliss at *The Hit or
      Miss* [1]
  We had drunk — not a penny left;
What then we did — well, now 'tis hid, —
  But better we'd stooped to theft!

[1] An old tavern now demolished.   The full legend over
the door ran, " Hit or Miss: Luck's All ! "

NO BELL–RINGING

"Yet, since none other remains who can,
   And few more years are mine,
I may tell you," said the cramped old man.
   "We — swilled the Sacrament-wine.

"Then each set-to with the strength of two,
   Every man to his bell ;
But something was wrong we found ere long
   Though what, we could not tell.

"We pulled till the sweat-drops fell around,
   As we'd never pulled before,
An hour by the clock, but not one sound
   Came down through the bell-loft floor.

"On the morrow all folk of the same thing
     spoke,
   They had stood at the midnight time
On their doorsteps near with a listening ear,
   But there reached them never a chime.

"We then could read the dye of our deed,
   And we knew we were accurst ;
But we broke to none the thing we had
     done,
   And since then never durst."

"I LOOKED BACK"

I LOOKED back as I left the house,
   And past the chimneys and neighbour
      tree.
The moon upsidled through the boughs: —
I thought: "I shall a last time see
This picture; when will that time be?"

I paused amid the laugh-loud feast,
And selfward said: "I am sitting where,
Some night, when ancient songs have ceased,
'Now is the last time I shall share
Such cheer,'" will be the thought I bear.

An eye-sweep back at a look-out corner
Upon a hill, as forenight wore,
Stirred me to think: "Ought I to warn her
That, though I come here times three-score,
One day 'twill be I come no more?"

Anon I reasoned there had been,
Ere quite forsaken was each spot,
Bygones whereon I'd lastly seen
That house, that feast, that maid forgot;
But when? — Ah, I remembered not!

THE AGED NEWSPAPER
SOLILOQUIZES

YES; yes; I am old.   In me appears
   The history of a hundred years;
Empires', kings', captives', births and deaths,
Strange faiths, and fleeting shibboleths.
— Tragedy, comedy, throngs my page
Beyond all mummed on any stage:
Cold hearts beat hot, hot hearts beat cold,
And I beat on.   Yes; yes; I am old.

CHRISTMAS: 1924

"PEACE upon earth!" was said. We
        sing it,
And pay a million priests to bring it.
After two thousand years of mass
We've got as far as poison-gas.

1924.

THE SINGLE WITNESS

"DID no one else, then, see them, man,
        Lying among the whin?
Did no one else, behold them at all
        Commit this shameless sin,
But you, in the hollow of the down
        No traveller's eye takes in?"

"Nobody else, my noble lord,
        Saw them together there —
Your young son's tutor and she. I made
        A short cut from the fair,
And lit on them. I've said no word
        About it anywhere."

"Good. . . . Now, you see my father's sword,
        Hanging up in your view;
No hand has swung it since he came
        Home after Waterloo.
I'll show it you. . . . There is the sword:
        And this is what I'll do."

He ran the other through the breast,
        Ere he could plead or cry.
"It is a dire necessity,
        But — since no one was nigh
Save you and they, my historied name
        Must not be smirched thereby."

HOW SHE WENT TO IRELAND

DORA'S gone to Ireland
　　Through the sleet and snow;
Promptly she has gone there
　　In a ship, although
Why she's gone to Ireland
　　Dora does not know.

That was where, yea, Ireland,
　　Dora wished to be:
When she felt, in lone times,
　　Shoots of misery,
Often there, in Ireland,
　　Dora wished to be.

Hence she's gone to Ireland,
　　Since she meant to go,
Through the drift and darkness
　　Onward labouring, though
That she's gone to Ireland
　　Dora does not know.

DEAD "WESSEX" THE DOG TO THE HOUSEHOLD

DO you think of me at all,
    Wistful ones?
Do you think of me at all
    As if nigh?
Do you think of me at all
At the creep of evenfall,
Or when the sky-birds call
    As they fly?

Do you look for me at times,
    Wistful ones?
Do you look for me at times
    Strained and still?
Do you look for me at times,
When the hour for walking chimes,
On that grassy path that climbs
    Up the hill?

You may hear a jump or trot,
    Wistful ones,
You may hear a jump or trot —
    Mine, as 'twere —

159

DEAD "WESSEX"

You may hear a jump or trot
On the stair or path or plot;
But I shall cause it not,
    Be not there.

Should you call as when I knew you,
    Wistful ones,
Should you call as when I knew you,
    Shared your home;
Should you call as when I knew you,
I shall not turn to view you,
I shall not listen to you,
    Shall not come.

THE WOMAN WHO WENT EAST

"WHERE is that woman of the west,
    Good Sir, once friends with me,
In rays of her own rareness drest,
And fired by sunset from the sea?
    Yes, she — once friends with me."

"— She went to sojourn in the east,
    O stranger Dame, one day;
Her own west land she reckoned least
Of all lands, with its weird old way,
    So left it, Dame, one day:

"Doubtless they prized her marvellous mould
    At its right worth elsewhere,
Yea, Dame, and kept her shrined in gold,
So speaking, as one past compare;
    Aye, prized her worth elsewhere!"

"— Must, must I then a story tell,
    Old native, here to you,
Of peradventures that befel
Her eastward — shape it as 'twere new,
    Old native, here to you?

161

THE WOMAN WHO WENT EAST

"O unforgotten day long back,
  When, wilful, east she sped
From you with her new Love. Alack,
Her lips would still be ripe and red
  Had she not eastward sped!

"For know, old lover, dull of eyes,
  That woman, I am she:
This skeleton that Time so tries
Your rose of rareness used to be;
  Yes, sweetheart, I am she."

NOT KNOWN

THEY know the wilings of the world,
    The latest flippancy;
They know each jest at hazard hurled,
    But know not me.

They know a phasm they name as me,
    In whom I should not find
A single self-held quality
    Of body or mind.

THE BOY'S DREAM

PROVINCIAL town-boy he, — frail, lame,
    His face a waning lily-white,
A court the home of his wry, wrenched frame,
Where noontide shed no warmth or light.

Over his temples — flat, and wan,
Where bluest veins were patterned keen,
The skin appeared so thinly drawn
The skull beneath was almost seen.

Always a wishful, absent look
Expressed it in his face and eye;
At the strong shape this longing took
One guessed what wish must underlie.

But no.   That wish was not for strength,
For other boys' agility,
To race with ease the field's far length,
Now hopped across so painfully.

He minded not his lameness much,
To shine at feats he did not long,
Nor to be best at goal and touch,
Nor at assaults to stand up strong.

THE BOY'S DREAM

But sometimes he would let be known
What the wish was : — to have, next spring,
A real green linnet — his very own —
Like that one he had late heard sing.

And as he breathed the cherished dream
To those whose secrecy was sworn,
His face was beautified by the theme,
And wore the radiance of the morn.

THE GAP IN THE WHITE

(178-)

SOMETHING had cracked in her mouth
        as she slept,
Having danced with the Prince long, and
        sipped his gold tass;
And she woke in alarm, and quick, breath-
        lessly, leapt
    Out of bed to the glass.

And there, in the blue dawn, her mouth now
        displayed
    To her woe, in the white
Level line of her teeth, a black gap she had
        made
    In a dream's nervous bite.

"O how can I meet him to-morrow!" she
        said.
"I'd won him — yes, yes! Now, alas, he
        is lost!"
(That age knew no remedy.) Duly her
        dread
    Proved the truth, to her cost.

THE GAP IN THE WHITE

And if you could go and examine her grave
    You'd find the gap there,
But not understand, now that science can
    save,
    Her unbounded despair.

FAMILY PORTRAITS

THREE picture-drawn people stepped out
  of their frames —
    The blast, how it blew!
And the white-shrouded candles flapped
    smoke-headed flames;
— Three picture-drawn people came down
    from their frames,
And dumbly in lippings they told me their
    names,
      Full well though I knew.

The first was a maiden of mild wistful tone,
      Gone silent for years,
The next a dark woman in former time
    known;
But the first one, the maiden of mild wistful
    tone,
So wondering, unpractised, so vague and
    alone,
      Nigh moved me to tears.

The third was a sad man — a man of much
    gloom;
      And before me they passed
In the shade of the night, at the back of the
    room,

FAMILY PORTRAITS

The dark and fair woman, the man of much
     gloom,
Three persons, in far-off years forceful, but
     whom
    Death now fettered fast.

They set about acting some drama, obscure,
    The women and he,
With puppet-like movements of mute strange
     allure;
Yea, set about acting some drama, obscure,
Till I saw 'twas their own lifetime's tragic
     amour,
    Whose course begot me;

Yea — a mystery, ancestral, long hid from
     my reach
    In the perished years past,
That had mounted to dark doings each
     against each
In those ancestors' days, and long hid from
     my reach;
Which their restless enghostings, it seemed,
     were to teach
    Me in full, at this last.

But fear fell upon me like frost, of some hurt
    If they entered anew

On the orbits they smartly had swept when
    expert
In the law-lacking passions of life, — of some
    hurt
To their souls — and thus mine — which I
    fain would avert;
    So, in sweat cold as dew,

"Why wake up all this?" I cried out.
     "Now, so late!
    Let old ghosts be laid!"
And they stiffened, drew back to their frames
    and numb state,
Gibbering: "Thus are your own ways to
    shape, know too late!"
Then I grieved that I'd not had the courage
    to wait
    And see the play played.

I have grieved ever since: to have balked
    future pain,
    My blood's tendance foreknown,
Had been triumph. Nights long stretched
    awake I have lain
Perplexed in endeavours to balk future pain
By uncovering the drift of their drama. In
    vain,
    Though therein lay my own.

THE CATCHING BALLET OF THE
WEDDING CLOTHES

(Temp. Guliel. IV.)

" A GENTLEMAN'S coming
         To court me, they say;
The ringers are told,
     And the band is to play.
O why should he do it
     Now poor Jack's away?
I surely shall rue it:
     Come, white witch, and say!"

"The gentleman's coming
     To marry you, dear;
They tell at the turnpikes
     That he has been here!
He rode here in secret,
     To gain eye of you: —
Throw over the sailor,
     Is what I should do!"

"I will not throw over
     Poor Jack: no, indeed,
For a new unknown lover
     Who loves at such speed,

171

And writes to the ringers,
   And orders the band,
As if I could only
   Obey his command!

"La! now here is something
   Close packed in a box,
And strapped up and corded,
   And held with two locks!"
"Dear, that's from him, surely,
   As we may suppose?
Ay, through the chink shining
   I spy wedding clothes!"

"Yes — here's a drawn bonnet,
   And tortoiseshell combs,
And a silk gown, silk stockings,
   And scents of rare blooms;
And shoes, too, of satin,
   Quite past all my pride:
O, how will it end, witch;
   I can't be his bride!"

"Don't waste you in weeping:
   Not worth it is man!
Beshrew me, my deary,
   I've shaped a new plan.
Wear the clothes of the rich one,
   Since he will not see,

But marry the poor one
    You love faithfully."

"Here's a last packet. . . . Never!
    It knocks me to bits —
The ring! '*Just to try on,*
    To see if it fits.'
O I cannot!" . . . But Jack said,
    Quite cool, when he came,
"Well, it will save money,
    And be just the same."

The marriage took place,
    Yes; as vowed, she was true
To her dear sailor Jack
    Ere the gentleman knew;
But she wore the rich clothing,
    Much joyed at such guise,
Yet fearing and trembling
    With tears in her eyes.

And at midnight, between her
    And him she had wed,
The gentleman's figure
    Arose up and said:
"My too-cruel darling,
    In spite of your oaths,
You have married the man
    Of the ring and the clothes!"

Thence on, would confront her,
　　When sleep had grown slack,
His face on the pillow
　　Between her and Jack;
And he nightly kept whispering:
　　"You surely must see,
Though your tongue-tip took him, Love,
　　Your body took me."

Till she sighed: "Yes, my word,
　　It must be confessed o' me,
Jack has; but this man
　　Can claim all the rest o' me!
And off to go with him
　　Bewitched am I now:
I'd fain not be two men's,
　　And won't, anyhow!"

So she pleaded and pleaded
　　From daybreak till dark,
Converting the parish
　　(Save parson and clerk.)
She then wrote to Jack thus:
　　"I'm torn with mind-strife:
She who wears a man's bride-clothes
　　Must be the man's wife!"

And still she kept plaining,
　　Till Jack he wrote: "Aye!"

174

And the villagers gathered,
   And, on a fixed day,
They went out alertly
   And stood in a row,
Quite blithe with excitement
   To see John's wife go.

Some were facing her dwelling,
   And some on the bridge,
And some at the corner,
   And some by the ridge.
With a nod and a word
   The coach stopped at her door,
And she upped like a bird,
   And they saw her no more.

'Twas told that, years after,
   When autumn winds wave,
A wealthy old lady
   Stood long at Jack's grave,
The while her coach waited : —
   She mused there ; and then
She stepped in, and never
   Came thither again.

1919.

175

A WINSOME WOMAN

SONG

THERE'S no winsome woman so win-
    some as she;
    Some are flower-like in mouth,
    Some have fire in the eyes,
    Some feed a soul's drouth
    Trilling words music-wise;
But where are these gifts all in one found to
    be
    Save in her known to me?

What her thoughts are I read not, but this
    much I know,
    That she, too, will pass
    From the sun and the air
    To her cave under grass;
    And the world will declare,
"No such woman as his passioned utterances
    show
    Walked this planet, we trow!"

THE BALLAD OF LOVE'S SKELETON

(179–)

"COME, let's to Culliford Hill and Wood,
    And watch the squirrels climb,
And look in sunny places there
    For shepherds' thyme."

— "Can I have heart for Culliford Wood,
    And hill and bank and tree,
Who know and ponder over all
    Things done by me!"

— "Then Dear, don hat, and come along :
    We'll strut the Royal strand ;
King George has just arrived, his Court,
    His guards, and band."

— "You are a Baron of the King's Court
    From Hanover lately come,
And can forget in song and dance
    What chills me numb.

177

THE BALLAD OF LOVE'S SKELETON

"Well be the royal scenes for you,
　　And band beyond compare,
But how is she who hates her crime
　　　To frolic there?

"O why did you so urge and say
　　'Twould soil your noble name!—
I should have prized a little child,
　　　And faced the shame.

"I see the child — *that should have been,*
　　But was not, born alive;
With such a deed in a woman's life
　　　A year seems five.

"I asked not for the wifely rank,
　　Nor maiden honour saved;
To call a nestling thing my own
　　　Was all I craved.

"For what's the hurt of shame to one
　　Of no more note than me?
Can littlest life beneath the sun
　　　More littled be?"

—"Nay, never grieve.　The day is bright,
　　Just as it was ere then:
In the Assembly Rooms to-night
　　　Let's joy again!

THE BALLAD OF LOVE'S SKELETON

"The new Quick-Step is the sweetest dance
  For lively toes and heels;
And when we tire of that we'll prance
  Bewitching reels.

"Dear, never grieve! As once we whirled
  So let us whirl to-night,
Forgetting all things save ourselves
  Till dawning light.

"The King and Queen, Princesses three,
  Have promised to meet there
The mayor and townsfolk. I've my card
  And One to spare.

"The Court will dance at the upper end;
  Only a cord between
Them and the burgher-throng below;
  A brilliant scene!"

— "I'll go. You've still my heart in thrall:
  Save you, all's dark to me.
And God knows what, when love is all,
  The end will be!"

A PRIVATE MAN ON PUBLIC MEN

WHEN my contemporaries were driving
    Their coach through Life with strain
    and striving,
And raking riches into heaps,
And ably pleading in the Courts
With smart rejoinders and retorts,
Or where the Senate nightly keeps
Its vigils, till their fames were fanned
By rumour's tongue throughout the land,
I lived in quiet, screened, unknown,
Pondering upon some stick or stone,
Or news of some rare book or bird
Latterly bought, or seen, or heard,
Not wishing ever to set eyes on
The surging crowd beyond the horizon,
Tasting years of moderate gladness
Mellowed by sundry days of sadness,
Shut from the noise of the world without,
Hearing but dimly its rush and rout,
Unenvying those amid its roar,
Little endowed, not wanting more.

CHRISTMAS IN THE ELGIN ROOM

BRITISH MUSEUM : EARLY LAST CENTURY

"WHAT is the noise that shakes the night,
    And seems to soar to the Pole-star
    height?"
    — "Christmas bells,
    The watchman tells
Who walks this hall that blears us captives
    with its blight."

"And what, then, mean such clangs, so
    clear?"
"— 'Tis said to have been a day of cheer,
    And source of grace
    To the human race
Lone ere their woven sails winged us to exile
    here.

"We are those whom Christmas overthrew
Some centuries after Pheidias knew
    How to shape us
    And bedrape us
And to set us in Athena's temple for men's
    view.

CHRISTMAS IN THE ELGIN ROOM

"O it is sad now we are sold —
We gods! for Borean people's gold,
    And brought to the gloom
    Of this gaunt room
Which sunlight shuns, and sweet Aurore but
    enters cold.

"For all these bells, would I were still
Radiant as on Athenai's Hill."
    — "And I, and I!"
    The others sigh,
"Before this Christ was known, and we had
    men's good will."

Thereat old Helios could but nod,
Throbbed, too, the Ilissus River-god,
    And the torsos there
    Of deities fair,
Whose limbs were shards beneath some Acro-
    politan clod:

Demeter too, Poseidon hoar,
Persephone, and many more
    Of Zeus' high breed, —
    All loth to heed
What the bells sang that night which shook
    them to the core.

1905 and 1926.

"WE ARE GETTING TO THE END"

WE are getting to the end of visioning
    The impossible within this universe,
Such as that better whiles may follow worse,
And that our race may mend by reasoning.

We know that even as larks in cages sing
Unthoughtful of deliverance from the curse
That holds them lifelong in a latticed hearse,
We ply spasmodically our pleasuring.

And that when nations set them to lay waste
Their neighbours' heritage by foot and horse,
And hack their pleasant plains in festering
    seams,
They may again, — not warely, or from taste,
But tickled mad by some demonic force. —
Yes. We are getting to the end of dreams!

HE RESOLVES TO SAY NO MORE

O MY soul, keep the rest unknown!
It is too like a sound of moan
When the charnel-eyed
Pale Horse has nighed:
Yea, none shall gather what I hide!

Why load men's minds with more to bear
That bear already ails to spare?
From now alway
Till my last day
What I discern I will not say.

Let Time roll backward if it will;
(Magians who drive the midnight quill
With brain aglow
Can see it so,)
What I have learnt no man shall know.

And if my vision range beyond
The blinkered sight of souls in bond,
— By truth made free —
I'll let all be,
And show to no man what I see.